IMAGES OF ENGLAND

# HORSFORTH

A view over Horsforth, c. 1930s.

IMAGES OF ENGLAND

# HORSFORTH

ALAN COCKROFT & MATTHEW YOUNG

TEMPUS

First published 1995
Reprinted 2004

Tempus Publishing Limited
The Mill, Brimscombe Port,
Stroud, Gloucestershire, GL5 2QG
www.tempus-publishing.com

British Library Cataloguing in Publication Data.
A catalogue record for this book is available from the British Library.

ISBN 0 7524 0130 0

Typesetting and origination by Tempus Publishing Limited.
Printed in Great Britain.

Workers building the ring road in the 1930s.

# Contents

# Acknowledgements

Many thanks must go to all those who lent pictures and postcards and offered information. In particular, the contributions of David Hey, Norman Pratt and Don Mitchell were invaluable; the cricketing statistics were generously provided by Roger Young. Thanks must also go to Marjorie Cockroft (and the dogs) for their patience.

Mistakes or factual errors in the book are entirely the fault of the authors but we would appreciate and welcome any further information concerning the photographs featured here. Anyone interested in pursuing Horsforth's History will find excellent documented collections at the Library and the Horsforth Village Museum.

Horsforth Hall Park Cricket Club, 1920 – champions of the Airdale and Wharfedale League. The player on the far right (sitting) is wearing a Yorkshire County Cricket club cap but has not yet been identified.

# Introduction

The photographs in this collection, the majority previously unpublished, span from the nineteenth century to recent times and chart the transformation that Horsforth has undergone. The book is a progression showing the rise and decline of the Mill industries; the expansion of the rail network; creeping urbanisation and its necessary accomplice, the motor car; rationalisation of education and the growth of consumerism. A century's change may be sweeping but the camera illuminates the detail and captures in an instant the very essence of time and place: the fashions, the shops, the homes, the workplace. The easy pace of the life presented here may have vanished but these pictures provide a thread to the past and are a part of our heritage. Everyone who lives or works in the area will recognise streets, buildings or even faces and the dramatic change that has been wrought in such a short span of history.

Today, Horsforth is a bustling conurbation of the giant sprawl that constitutes Metropolitan Leeds. Yet for many older residents Horsforth retains many of the qualities of village life a distinct entity and a real sense of community. These feelings may be attributed to Horsforth's geographical isolation – it is essentially an island. The River Aire and the Becks of Gill and Moseley (Oil Mill) form a natural boundary. Saxon travellers passing through Horsforth would have to cross water and the name given to the area by the Normans in the Domesday Book was Horseforde, a natural crossing point for livestock and people. The ancient ford was probably situated at Newlay but documentation is not specific and could refer to numerous accessible crossing points within the area.

Before 1066 the Horsforth area was held by three Saxon nobles but after the Norman Conquest these lands were given to members of William I retinue, as was custom, for military or civil service. Land was the currency of the day and England, a conquered territory, was carved up between the Earls, Lords and knights of Normandy. The Saxon nobility were simply dispossessed. Horsforth became a feudal fief of Robert de Bruis, Robert de Rouilly and the Percy family.

During the Twelfth Century the manor of Horsforth came under the influence of the Mauleverer family. A steward of Ralph Mauleverer, Nigel de Horisford, collected the feudal due or rent from the tenants of Horsforth although this sum was not enough to give Nigel the status of knight. Nigel had undoubtley taken his name from the settlement although the spelling varies in documents. At this time the monks of Barnoldswick had begun the building of Kirkstall Abbey; Nigel supplied much of the building material as well as the original site. The link between the Abbey and Horsforth had been established and would grow stronger: regular gifts of land, money and materials were given and by the Fourteenth Century the Abbey would possess two-thirds of Horsforth lands.

It was during this period that Hugh de Horisford was probably approached by a member of the Abbey with the idea of building a chapel on what is today Chapel Green. The notion of a family chapel for local nobility was already normal practice and would have appealed to Hugh. The original chapel is no longer standing but the centre of Horsforth had been established. Around the chapel a collection of weavers cottages would have grown (organised by monks from the Abbey) and a tavern erected to cater for thirsty workers. The monks also build a tithe barn (c.1150s), the site of the present Newlaithes Manor, for tenants to supply their dues in the form of part of the annual harvest and were responsible for the maintenance of the Granges around the area.

After the Dissolution of the Monasteries the lands of Horsforth passed into the hands of several families. The most notable amongst these were the Stanhopes: the founders of Horsforth Hall; patrons of St. Margarets church and owners of local industry. The Stanhope family and the early history of Horsforth are tied. Patronage and gifts gave Horsforth much of its contemporary shape.

This is also a story of Horsforth folk: a tough and hardy breed who gave meaning to the maxim 'work hard, play hard'. Horsforth people were undoubtedly thirsty. The numerous public houses in Horsforth were often the second home (and sometimes the first) to many local workers providing an outlet from the grind of hard labour. This gritty determination is also featured in the numerous sporting teams: several Yorkshire (and England) cricketers learnt their trade on the park at Horsforth Hall; Woodside Wanderers battled away in the Red Triangle League; the bowling clubs brought home several regional championships.

These pictures demonstrate that Horsforth, despite becoming part of a metropolitan area, has a community that remains resolutely independent: an independence firmly grounded in the past.

Matthew Young
January 1995


In my years of living in Horsforth there have been vast changes. The open fields and surrounding farms have gone. As children we led almost a rural life: we caught stickle backs (tiddlers) in Woodside Beck; swam in Fleggy Beck by the Station and caught trout all the way up to Bramhope Tunnel. Kingfishers, Herons and Dippers could be seen all over Oil Mill Beck. I started school at Providence in Broadgate Lane and if you looked back up the hill all you could see were cornfields; at night you would hear Corncrates calling. The areas around Station Road, Sussex Avenue, Brownberries and Hungerhills were, not so long ago, grazing land. When we queued for the Imperial Pictures on Town Street we used to watch the cows being milked after they had been brought off the Dilly Fields or as we knew it Feast Field.

I hope by these few words I managed to express why in some ways I feel so sad at what the speculators have done to the village but I hope that this book gives those new to Horsforth an interesting glimpse of a past time and brings back many memories to those older ones who were born here.

Alan Cockroft
January 1995

# *One*
# Rural Horsforth

A modern view of Kirkstall Abbey. The Abbey was founded in 1132 by monks from Barnoldswick. The original site was a gift from the de Horisford family. The influence of the Abbey over the Horsforth area remained unchallenged until Dissolution in the Sixteenth Century.

A modern view of St. Margaret's Church. The project to build the church was undertaken in 1873 as the Bell Chapel was proving inadequate for the needs of parishoners. Land was donated by the Stanhope Family and the Church was consecrated on December, 8th 1883 at a cost of £13,000. The original funds however did not cover the cost of a spire which was added in 1901.

St. Margaret's Church, c. 1950. This picture would have been taken from somewhere along Hall Lane and looks up toward Hunger Hills. On the right is Church Road.

Grove Wesleyans Cricket Team in the open fields surrounding the Church, c. 1930s. Cragg Baptists also played matches here.

A recent view of Hunger Hills and Hall Park Estates c. 1994, looking towards the centre of Leeds.

The fields beside Hall Lane, *c.* 1950s. The horses belonged to Hutchinson's farm.

Bluebell Woods in 1950. The path leads up to Hunger Hills.

The site of the present Hunger Hills Estate looking toward Hall Lane and Pudsey. This rustic scene is from the 1930s.

Church Road, *c.* 1925.

The construction of the new relief road in the 1960s. The road was built as a relief for Town Street.

The top of Hall Lane, c. 1930

Quaker Hall on Hall Lane, *c*. 1910. This building was later to become the Horsforth Ex-Servicemen's Club. The inscription above the entrance read: 'God is Love'.

The corner of Hall Lane and West End Lane, *c*. 1910. Part of the house on the right was removed during subsequent road alterations.

Claygate Farm on Hall Lane, *c.* 1920, when the Lane was an unmade road.

Hall Park cricket team performing during the 1950s. Many famous players displayed their talents on the park, including Sir Len Hutton, Bill Bowes and Herbert Sutcliffe. A scorebook exists for the Hall Park club from 1894 and it is probable that the club was formed at around this time as the ownership of Horsforth Hall came into the hands of Sir William Duncan in 1891, allowing the creation of a wicket in the park.

Horsforth Hall, formerly family home to the Stanhope family, *c.* 1937. John Stanhope IV commissioned the Hall (originally called New Hall) to be built in 1699 and the final completions were made in 1707; the family were at that time living at Low Hall. The Hall was let in 1806.

Horsforth Hall, *c.* 1950s.

Horsforth Hall Park during the Coronation celebrations, 1953.

Low Hall, c. 1910, the original home of the Stanhope family. The Hall originally belonged to the Greene family who were direct descendants of the de Horisford family. There was bitter rivalry between the Stanhopes and the Greenes. The Stanhopes, through their thrifty nature, eventually forced Michael Greene (who had inherited a rapidly escalating debt) to sell part of the Hall and its accompanying estate in 1628. The Greene family moved away from the Horsforth area soon after.

Low Hall Farm, *c.* 1950.

A drawing of Newlaithes Hall.

Newlaithes Manor, *c.* 1950. The building, now listed, has since passed through several owners hands. The Manor is reputedly the oldest building within Horsforth, being constructed as a 'tithe barn' in 1154. The original structure of wood with walls of mud and wattle was replaced in the fifteenth century; much of the internal panelling is original. During the Dissolution of the Monasteries local legend stated that monks from Kirkstall Abbey hid gold within the walls. Some later owners have been known to spend days tapping the panels for secret compartments that would lead to a fortune.

Newlaithes Manor, *c.* 1970.

Low Fold Farm, *c*. 1920s. The farm was bought by Samuel Swaine in the 1630s and subsequent documents have described it as 'a manor'. It is possible that an old house existed at the site but a credible explanation is that it was a part of the landed estate (manor) of the Calverley family during the division of lands between five Horsforth families. John Wesley preached at the farm in 1786.

Throstle Nest Farmhouse, *c*. 1910, was constructed in the eighteenth century. It was originally the 'Laithe' or barn with a cottage adjoining. The building was saved from demolition by Horsforth Civic Society in 1972 after W.R.C.C. refused to grant a preservation order.

A view overlooking Tinshill in the 1920s.

*Two*

# The Green

A photograph of an original painting of the Old Bell Chapel. The artist and date are unknown.

The Bell Chapel in the 1880s. The site of the chapel was originally given as a gift by Hugh de Horisford to monks of Kirkstall Abbey in the Twelfth Century. John Wesley preached at the chapel in 1786 and the last sermon was held on December, 2nd 1883. The building began to be pulled down in 1885. Although the chapel is no longer standing the foundations can still be seen. The Chapel and the Green are the original centre of Horsforth.

The Blackbull Inn on the corner of the Green in 1873. The building became a Public House in 1758 under the stewardship of Jim Lapish.

The Blackbull Inn, *c.* 1910. From the number of regulars it seems to have maintained its popularity.

The corner of the Green in the 1950s.

The edge of the Bell Chapel wall on the right, *c.* 1900.

The Green with St. Margaret's hall on the right.

The Green, c. 1880s.

The Butcher's Shop on Chapel Green in the 1930s. From left to right are Jim Myers, Samuel Myers and Jack Myers.

The Old Kings Arms on Chapel Green in 1924. The proprietress at this time was Ada Chapman. The building became a Public House in 1749.

The entrance to Horsforth Hall Park from Willow Green, *c.* 1910. This is now the site of the Leeds ring road.

Fink Hill, *c.* 1920. The house on the left is 'The Willows' and the approaching car appears to be a Ford Model 'T'.

The top of Fink Hill looking toward Chapel Green, *c.* 1930s.

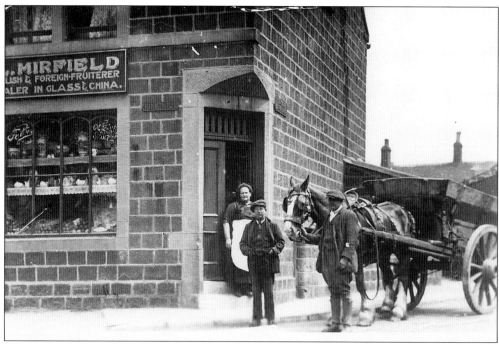

Mirfield's General Stores on Willow Green, *c.* 1920s.

The Stanhope Arms in 1907. The landlord pictured here is Charles Howett. In the 1920s the pub was bought by a brewery, Hammond's Fountain Brewery of Bradford, and was eventually purchased by Bass in 1970.

The Eleventh Earl (formerly the Stanhope Arms) in the 1980s. The name was changed to avoid confusion with the Stanhope Hotel.

# *Three*

# Town Street and Long Row

The Old Kings Arms in the 1980s. The pub was opened in 1749 and the first landlord was a Mr James Lambert.

A view from the bottom of Town Street during the 1920s.

Town Street, *c.* 1907.

The Salvation Army building in 1960. The building, which was situated on lower Town Street, was demolished just ten years later. For many years the building was home to the 'Copper Kettle Cafe'.

The Old Arcade in 1910. The shop on the bottom right was Walkers, which sold postcards and stationery. Moving up the Arcade the other premises were: the Yorkshire Penny Bank; Whitfields; the Post Office (under the control of Miss Hutchinson); Mr Lee's, a barbers which later became Wilson's Flower shop, and Bonners Shoe Shop.

Tithe Cottage on Town Street in the 1950s. The cottage was used to accommodate local clergy. Sadly, the cottage was demolished to make way for the shopping complex which bears its name.

The centre of Town Street in 1910. The Co-operative Store on the left was directly opposite Dicky Barratt's Clock Shop.

The Co-op Butchers in 1933. From left to write they are Jack Hogg, Harry Chadwick, Jack Briggs and Stan Sheldon.

The centre of Town Street in the early 1950s.

A.S. Armitage Engineers and Electrical Shop during the 1930s. Stan Sheldon, the Co-operative delivery boy, appears to have his eye on a possible bargain.

A modern view of Town Street in the 1980s during continuing rebuilding.

Bonners Shoe Shop in the early 1960s. The shop moved to these premises from the Old Arcade in 1917. Today, the National Provincial are the occupants.

Terraced housing in the 1960s which was demolished to make way for shops. The site, however, remains empty.

Town Street in the late 1960s. These terraces have all since been demolished but one was owned by Mrs Arthington, a venerable and formidable lady who, upon the delivery under the door of her rates bill, would use bellows to blow the accursed bill back out. Upon reporting back to his office, the council official responsible was heard to comment, 'I don't think I'd pay my rates if I lived in such a drafty house.'

A view toward Quarry Bank, *c.* 1930.

Town Street in the late 1950s. The garage on the right was known as 'Smalls' but was later sold to J.E. Cassers.

Middle of Town Street in 1920. On the right is G.E. Smith's opticians.

A view of Stables Drapery in Town Street at the turn of the century.

York City and County Bank Company Ltd, *c.* 1900. The York Company had the first banking offices in Horsforth when they purchased this building in Town Street in 1895. The Midland maintained a branch in the Old Arcade from 1901. The first branch manager of the York City Bank was Ernest Newman but in 1909 the company was bought by the London Joint Stock Bank which became part of the Midland Bank in 1918.

Midland Bank in the 1980s. Despite several internal refurbishments the exterior of the building has remained unchanged.

The Mechanic's Institute on the corner of Town Street and Church Lane, c. 1912. The Institute, which is featured here with a flagpole, was originally situated at the Old Bell Chapel.

The Police Station and Mechanic's Institute in the 1960s. The alcove and fencing have been removed and the flagpole now resides by the Police Station. The station was eventually demolished to make way for the Library.

Town Street around 1900, with, on the right, Thomas Smales Cockroft's grocery shop, the Mechanics' Institute, police station, a milliner's shop and at the bottom the Crown Inn (later the Liberal Club).

Lane Head, c. 1910. On the left is the 'New Arcade' where Alfred Dibb sold quality leather goods and John Willy Thompson owned a greengrocers.

The Star and Garter Pub on Long Row in 1903. The pub's last Landlord William Marshall Tetley, his family and some regulars are shown.

A view of Well Cottage in 1970. The cottage was a chemist shop owned by Jack Carr but was sold to and refurbished by the Medimart Stores. One previous owner, known as 'Mother Duck', sold ground sandstone which when mixed with water formed a paste that cleaned most stone surfaces. The former Star and Garter Pub next door belonged to Jehovah's Witnesses in the 1970s but eventually became a solicitors office.

A view from the top of Batchelor Lane, *c.* 1900. The Grocery Store featured belonged to M.O. Grimshaw. The store once advertised that persons purchasing over 14lb of their blended teas would receive 'a splendid silver watch'.

Long Row, *c.* 1910. The shop on the right was Brown's, a hardware store.

Long Row in the 1950s. The old handloom weavers cottage in the centre was built with three storeys to accommodate the essential needs of a basic cottage industry living space, work place and storage.

Long Row, c. 1900. The buildings on the left were known as Dye House Cottages. It was here that handloom weavers would have brought their cloth to be coloured and dyed.

Long Row in the 1930s. The shop on the right belonged to F. Monks and sold footwear.

The corner of Station Road and Long Row in the late 1950s. Winnifride Mongan's sold ladies fashions.

The corner of Station Road and Long Row, c. 1910. The shop featured was a butchers belonging to E. Calverley.

# *Four*

# Woodside

Woodside, c. 1930s. Calder Tweed Mill can be seen in the background. The pub on the right is the Woolpack; the newsagents over the street is George Fairburn's, now owned by Chris Woods.

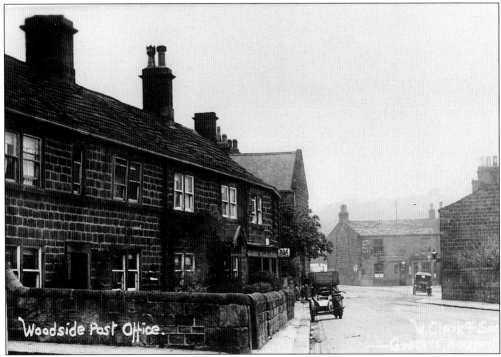

The bottom of Woodside by W.C. Clarke's Post office in the 1920s. At the bottom of the road is a Pickard's truck opposite the old Woodside Tavern.

Low Lane and Springfield Mount in the 1920s.

Broadgate Lane, *c.* 1952.

Ducks crossing Springfield Mount, *c.* 1930.

Butcher Hill on the eastern side of Oil Mill Beck, c. 1930.

A view over Woodside in the 1920s. At the bottom of the road is George Salmon with his fish barrow.

At the bottom of Tan House Hill beside the Bridge Inn, *c.* 1950.

MAPH (Ministry of Aircraft Production Houses), *c.* 1950. These houses were built (at great speed) during the Second World War to house workers from the A.V. Roe plant near Yeadon.

A view toward Low Lane from Broadgate, *c*. 1950.

The bottom of the Ring Road in 1950, before the junction became a roundabout.

Woodside and Cookridge, *c.* 1950s.

The Old Workhouse on Troy Hill, *c*. 1950. This mullion-windowed house was used as a workhouse from around the 1750s until 1795; this can be gathered from registers of burials. The entries suggest that the inmates also came from Rawdon. The building itself is much older – probably Tudor.

# *Five*

# Industry and Transport

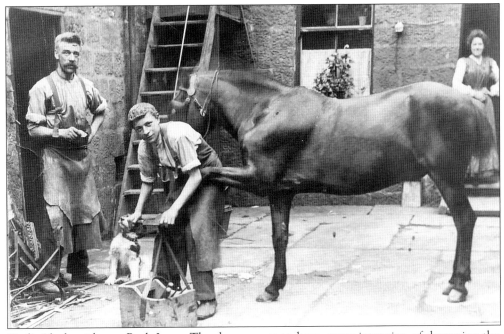

Peel's Blacksmiths on Back Lane. The dog appears to have every intention of devouring the owner's sandwich.

John Marsden's Blacksmiths on Long Row, c. 1930s. During the mid-eighteenth century Samuel Marsden, a native of the Horsforth area, worked here as a labourer before sailing to New South Wales in 1793 where he became the Chief Minister of the Anglican faith for the whole of the New Colony and was known as the 'floggerparson' for his harsh treatment of assigned convicts. He held substantial land around Parramatta, preached 'hellfire' sermons denouncing the Catholic faith, and published articles such as 'A Few Observations on the Toleration of the Catholic Religion in New South Wales'. Marsden was the first man in Australia to cross breed different types of Merino sheep creating the foundations for the colony's first great export.

R. Houseman, General Smiths, *c*. 1920s. The Smithy was situated on Woodside.

Nethersprings Bleach Works, *c*. 1900. The bleach works were founded by the Pullan family in the 1860s when the linen industry was at a peak. Flax, after the bleaching process, was dried upon a series of connected poles. The import of cheap American cotton toward the end of the century made many such industries redundant.

Mosley Pond House (or Moseley Bottom Pond), near Scotland Lane, *c.* 1920. A paper mill, belonging to William Craven, was also situated on the site.

The Manorial Corn Mill from a painting by David Hey. The site was a mill during the Dissolution, under the operating control of Richard Dawson, but was rebuilt several times. The mill was owned by Walter Stanhope in the eighteenth century but was linked to the Craven family who owned the next door cottage.

After the Great War the mill suffered from frequent 'blackouts' and 'shutdowns'. The solution, as employee Edwin Clarke remembered, was to place a six inch nail between the fuse box and the mains power supply.

Troy Mill in the early 1960s was owned by Hamlyn and Co. before its final demolition.

Ackroyd's Spinning Mill, Woodside, *c*. 1960.

The Brookfoot Mill Complex, Woodside, *c*. 1960. The original buildings, including a corn mill, cottages and a barn, date from the seventeenth century. A papermaking business was established in the last century by the Hague family. The site is currently known as the Bentley Soap Works which produces soaps for industrial usage. Thomas and John Bentley purchased the mill in 1896 moving their original business from the Station Yard. A part of the dam has since been partially filled.

Woodside (Cookridge) Silk Mill, *c*. 1950. During the heyday of the mill experienced workers were drawn here from Hebden Bridge and Halifax. A fire in 1873 gutted the original buildings and the site was not redeveloped until the 1880s under the ownership of John Charnley. Charnley was an enthusiast with little business sense and after several reorganisations the whole site was sold to Ainsworth Cloth in 1905.

The last owners of the Cookridge Mill site were Federick Wilson and Co. Ltd. (Dyers and Finishers). The site was demolished in the late 1970s.

The site of the present Dixon's Auto Village. The old silk mill is pictured in the background.

Calder Tweed or Woodside Mill, c. 1960s. The Mill was originally owned by Hutchinson and Company who produced high quality cloth. Unfortunately the company was also prosecuted under the regulations of the 1833 Factory Act for working children under eleven over sixty hours a week. The Calder Tweed Company purchased the Mill in 1917.

A modern view of Low Lane, looking towards the ring road; the site of the old Calder Tweed Mill.

The Tannery at Woodside in 1960. The industry at this site was started by James Watson at the beginning of the nineteenth century.

A view looking over to New Mill, *c.* 1950s. The oak bark stacked here was used in the tanning process.

A Lister Brothers and Company lorry in the 1930s.

The New Mill or 'Mathers' Mill', *c.* 1954. Built in 1903 for Mathers of Leeds as a worsted spinning plant, it was sold to Lister Brothers in 1927.

Workers inside Mathers Mill. The occasion is unknown.

A Wade's lorry in Horsforth, *c.* 1920s.

Whitakers Bros and Company delivery caravan, *c.* 1900.

A Throup and Sons gravel truck, *c*. 1930. The gravel was removed from Cragg Hill quarry.

A Whitakers Steam Crane, *c.* 1960s.

This particular steam crane was located at Musselburgh in Scotland and now resides in the local museum.

Bonner's shoe factory at the end of New Street, *c.* 1930s. The Bonner's shop was located on Town Street. The factory is reputed to have made the 'world's biggest boot'.

Horsforth Delivery Van, *c.* 1906. Herbert Naylor is holding the reins while Harold Ford is pictured sitting.

Mr Alan Holiday, son of the owner of Horsforth Super Laundry, *c*. 1918. The Holiday family bought the Laundry Service in 1910. In the background is the 'Tintabernacle' Imperial Picture House on Long Row which was demolished in the 1920s.

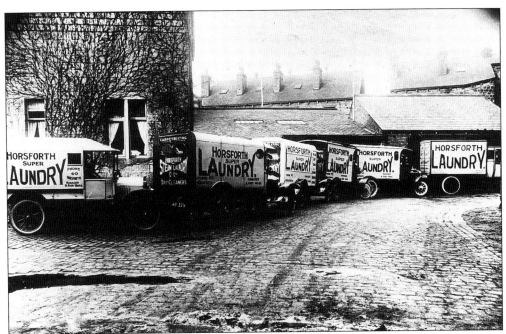

The Horsforth Super Laundry Van Depot at the top of Broadgate Lane, *c.* 1918. The Laundry was reputed to have the only fleet of Rolls Royces in the country.

The Horsforth Laundry Group fortieth celebrations. Pictured in the centre is Mr H. Mason, a member of the family who bought the company from the Holiday family.

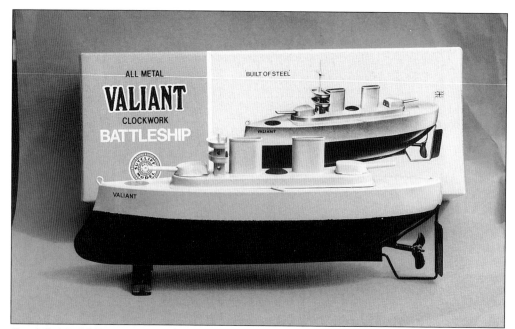

Sutcliffe Model Boats were produced in Horsforth for over sixty years and were sold worldwide; today they are a much sought after collectors item. The business was started in 1918 by J.W. Sutcliffe as a sideline to the products he made with tinplate. Many varieties of vessels were produced including a range of submarines. The business closed in 1981.

Workers from Sutcliffe Pressings Limited, c. 1950. The boats were produced at the Atlas Works (situated behind the present Midland Bank) which employed at its peak over thirty people. In the front is Cathleen Cockroft.

The old 'clapper' packhorse bridge as it crosses Oil Mill Beck; an ancient crossing point.

Calverley Mill Bridge in 1955. The bridge was built with funds from Sir Walter Calverley and John Stanhope IV in 1710 to cross the River Aire. The road that runs across the bridge was known as the Calverley and Horsforth Toll Road.

The Toll Gate at Calverley Bridge. Remembered by some locals as being 'twopence' to cross, the toll was rated at £30 per annum in 1882.

*Newlay Bridge, Horsforth.*

Newlay Bridge, *c.* 1900. This site may have been the original ford crossing that gave Horsforth its name. Built by John Pollard in 1819 the bridge was a very lucrative source of income in tolls.

The wooden footbridge over the River Aire at Newlay, *c.* 1910. The bridge was constructed in the 1880s by the Railway Company and the Horsforth Board to allow locals to cross without paying the toll at Newlay Bridge. After various legal actions the toll was 'freed' and the footbridge went into disrepair, eventually being pulled down in 1934.

The Toll House, Newlay Bridge, *c.* 1970.

Carr Bridge on Station Road, *c.* 1910.

The bridge near Dean Head on the Horsforth boundary, *c.* 1920.

The old Woolpack Bridge during the flood of September 1931.

A steam engine emerging from Bramhope Tunnel. The building of the tunnel was a great engineering feat but a financial and human disaster. Twenty-three workers were killed during its excavation and the budget was £1 million over the original estimates.

The bottom of Woodside, c. 1960s. The Fillingfir Estate is in the process of construction. Just beyond this point was the A.R. Briggs siding into the Quarry.

Station Road, *c.* 1920s.

Horsforth Station, *c.* 1930s.

Horsforth Station in the process of demolition during 1972.

Newlay and Horsforth Station in the 1950s. The station was closed ten years later.

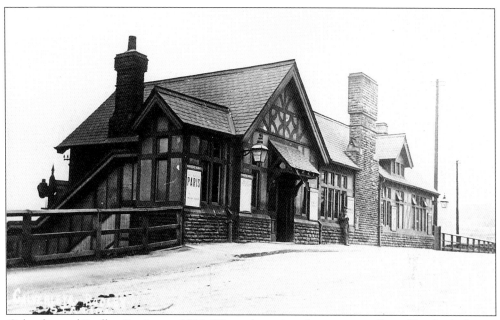

Calverley and Rodley Station, *c.* 1910. The only station that was actually in Horsforth. It was closed in 1965.

*The Yorkshireman* entering Horsforth.

The first electric tramcar to Horsforth as it stands at Calverley Lane May 16, 1906. The service, run by the Leeds Tramways, was extended into Yeadon and Guiseley three years later.

Manor Road, *c.* 1906.

Manor Road Corner in the 1980s. The council offices on the far left have recently been closed.

A regular bus service through Horsforth was operated by Sammy Ledgard from 1927 to 1967. Buses went to Otley and Ikley, Leeds and the surrounding areas. This picture is from the 1950s.

An original Sammy Ledgard bus from the 1930s outside the Nelson Hotel, Armley.

The Horsforth Road Sweepers, *c.* 1920.

The Leeds and Bradford Airport at Yeadon, *c.* 1950. The site was first used by the Yorkshire Aeroplane Club in the early 1930s but took on greater significance during the Second World War as a test site for the A.V. Roe planes produced nearby; these included the Lancaster bomber. Jet planes came to the Leeds and Bradford (International) Airport in 1984.

Hayes of Horsforth, a display for the Tyre Division, c. 1955.

Hayes of Horsforth in the 1960s. This building was used as the fire station during the war.

## Six

# Churches and Chapels

The Bell Chapel on the Green, c. 1870. It is possible to see the shape of a ghost in the doorway – perhaps a disgruntled member of the medieval clergy?

The Primitive Methodist Chapel on Town Street as it was being demolished in 1910.

Lister Hill Mission. The building was knocked down after the Second World War.

The Reverend Ford preaching inside the Lister Hill Mission in the late 1920s.

An artist's impression of the Methodist Ebenezer Chapel in 1881.

The Providence Chapel in Broadgate Lane, c. 1930. The building further from the camera was used as a junior school for many years.

Woodside Vicarage, Woodside, c. 1930. The house was built for the resident minister.

Woodside St. James's Church, *c*. 1920s. The church was constructed in 1847.

Woodside Methodist Church during construction in August 1894. Those identified are (from left to right): Mr Cummings, Miss Townsend, -?- , Ben Wilson, -?-, George Martin, Jasper Cummings, Mr Hibbard, William Dean, George Thompson (top), Harry Grant, Sam Lambert, Tom Lawrence (contractor), Harry Lupton (top), Noah Holden.

Zion Baptist Chapel, *c.* 1910. The name was later changed, the graveyard flattened and the chapel converted to its current use as a nursery school.

Cragg Hill Baptist Church, *c.* 1980, an excellent example of a handloom weavers cottage.

New Street School and Chapel, *c.* 1950, just before demolition to make way for a new housing estate.

Wesleyan Grove Chapel on Town Street, with Garden Street on the right, *c.* 1890s.

The participants of the first Confirmation service held at St. Margaret's Church, July 24th 1869. Those attending in descending order, left to right, were: Samuel Wood, John Wood, John William Dibb, Rev. Stocker, Joseph Wood, William Stables, Wilfred Lee, Joseph Hardaker, John Wade, J. Holgate, Edwin Riley, George Blythe, John Riley, K. Jillotson, J. Saxton, William Webster, J. Tordoff, James Dibb, Alfred Dibb, William Holmes, Samuel Ellis, Samuel Hewton, Joseph Swales, William Scott.

*Seven*

# Education

The old Town School, c. 1960s; the school has also been titled 'Horsforth National School'. Today it is the St. Margaret's Junior School.

New Council Schools in the 1930s, known locally as 'Featherbank'.

A 1930s class of Featherbank School.

The 1932 class of the Providence Infants School. Those identified so far are Alan Cockroft, Ken Smales and William Holdsworth. Ken Smales played cricket for Yorkshire and Nottinghamshire and is one of the few men in history to take ten wickets in an innings (10 for 66 versus Gloucestershire at Stroud in 1956). William Holdsworth played a season for Yorkshire in 1953 taking 32 wickets at the cost of 455 runs.

Horsforth National School, c. 1910

Woodside St. James School, *c.* 1910. The only person identified is Emma Foster (top left).

Class One of Horsforth National School, May 1925.

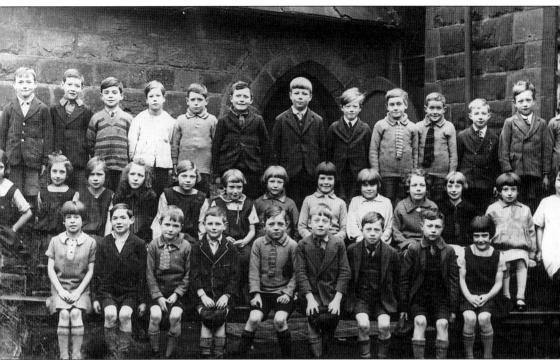

A National School Class in 1929. From left to right, top row: H. Gregory, C. Sheedy, N. Vesty, J. Graham, -?- , G. Salmon, G. Laurie, A. Yeadon, S. Riley, K. Riley, D. Leach, A. Swale, A. Dockery. Middle row: M. Tamms, P. Sanderson, J. Marsden, -?-, J. Thwaite, M. Morley, E. Wilkinson, L. Hirst, M. King, -?-, -?-, M. Riley, -?-. Front row: B. Maude, J. Dickenson, F. Padgett, J. Toft, J. Pickard, W. Knotingham, A. Foster, W. Stockhill, W. Pearson.

Froebelian School pupils, c. 1920s. This Co-educational School was founded in 1913 by Miss L. Hoe. The name 'Froebelian' is derived from Freidrich Wilhelm Froebel, the founder of the kindergarten system, whose educational methods based upon development through practical applications were popular in the 1840s.

The Froebelian School, c. 1920s. The original site for the school was the semi-detached houses opposite the present site on Clarence Road. In 1946 the school was sold to Mr and Mrs Williams and the site moved across the road to the present Mount building which was further extended in 1988. The present Headmaster is Mr John Andrew.

# *Eight*

# Sport and Leisure

Woodside Wanderers A.F.C., c. 1950s. The Wanderers were formed in 1947 by Peter Gee, Ronald Brown and Peter Atack as a junior (U18s) team and played at Horsforth Hall Park. The return of several servicemen from National Service prompted a change to senior level in 1953 and a new venue at Stanhope Drive. The team of that year won the First Division Championship of the Red Triangle League dropping only two points. In 1959 the club amalgamated with Horsforth Town and became the Horsforth Wanderers.

Horsforth Wanderers in the 1970s. Back row, left to right: Gerald Knight, Guy Summerton, Bill Turner, Ken Richardson, Alan Cook, Neil Cave, Steve Carter, Peter Read. Front row: David Hey, David Brookes, Graham Smith, Ian Senior, David Maud, Michael Reynolds.

A Horsforth Wanderers cartoon from 1960.

Hosforth A.F.C., 1930.

Horsforth Institute Cricket Club, *c.* 1910. From left to right, top row: G. Fairburn, W. Hurst, S. Riley, -?-, Wilf Pratt, B. Houseman, S. Stockhill, -?-, Harry Chambers. Middle row: George Fairburn, George Kirkby, Walter Chambers , H. Thompson, -?-. Front row: -?-, Harry Riley, -?-.

Horsforth Hall Park Cricket Club Second Eleven, 1925. Hedley Verity, described by many as the greatest ever bowler, played three seasons for the Hall Park Team during which he opened the bowling and the batting. His Yorkshire and England career was prestigious: he took ten wickets for ten runs against Nottinghamshire (including a hat-trick) in 1930; he snatched fourteen wickets in a day against Australia and played in over forty test matches. He was tragically killed in Italy in 1943 – with him at the time was another Horsforth man, Bob Marsden, who laid him to rest.

Woodside Comic Cricket Match, 1930.

Lister Hill Cricket Club, *c.* 1930s.

The ATC (Horsforth) Football Team, *c.* 1941. Those identified are 'Nobby' Clarke, Mr Kellett, Gavin Loudon, Mr Garnett, 'Pip' Walker, Ken Herd, Geoff Sharpe, Norman Mulkin, Peter Cobb, Ken Appleyard, Peter Reid, Jack Steel, Stan Johnson.

1311 Squadron Horsforth ATC band, c. 1941.

The Earl of Harewood inspects the ATC during the Second World War.

D Company of the 30th West Riding Home Guard outside St. Margaret's Church, October 1944.

Horsforth Air Raid Wardens, *c.* 1944.

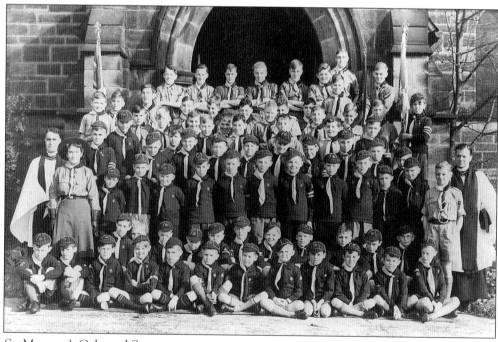

St. Margaret's Cubs and Scouts.

A refugee stall for Belgian Children during the Great War.

Horsforth Conscription Band, c. 1920s.

Woodside Tavern Bowling Club, *c.* 1930s. Horsforth used to boast several bowling teams, including The Black Bull and Horsforth Bridge. The remaining teams in the area are Horsforth Conservatives, Hall Park and Woodside. The Conservatives won the Yorkshire Cup (the premier title in the County) in 1977, 1978 and 1985; Woodside won the 'Henry Taylor' cup in 1927 and the Leeds Evening League in 1983 and 1984.

Broadway Hall, *c.* 1960s. The hall was the centre for the weekly dance in Horsforth.

A dance contest held inside Broadway Hall in the 1950s.

The St. Margaret's Church Choir on The Green, May Day 1920.

A bonfire at Woodside, *c.* 1950s.

Queuing for beer at The Ringway during rationing, 1940s.

The Old Ball Inn, c. 1955. The Inn was originally a farmhouse but became a Public House in 1773. Rumour insists that the pub derived its name from a misspelling of 'bull'.

The Fleece Hotel, c. 1910. The Proprietor at this time was John Houlden.

The Queens Arms on Long Row, *c.* 1910. This public house became a part of Bass in 1970. The pub is the oldest licensed building in Horsforth, but the Kings Arms has the distinction of holding the oldest licence.

# *Nine*

# Horsforth Views

Walter Stead's Cash Dividend Store at Fink Hill, *c.* 1920.

New Road Side General Supply Stores, *c.* 1910.

Mather Hutchinsons Butchers on Back Lane, *c.* 1890.

Charlie Rushton's Watch Shop on Town Street, *c.* 1960s.

Broadgate Parade, *c.* 1930s.

Patric Knowles, film and television star of many westerns, was born at Milton Cottage, Cripplesyke in 1911.

Broadway Hall in the 1920s. The Hall was known as 'Bank House'.

Featherbank outside 'The Friendly' (Horsforth Hotel), *c*. 1900.

Featherbank Lane and Abbey House at the turn of the century.

Leeds Work People's Hospital at Springfield, Dean Head. The house was used to house Bosnian Refugees after the break up of Yugoslavia but has recently been purchased by the Leeds and Bradford Airport.

Tea Rooms at Moorside, Scotland Lane, *c.* 1920s.

The murder of six year old Barbara Waterhouse in June 1891 shocked the residents of Horsforth. Her mutilated body (with over 45 wounds) was found in Leeds by a local constable. The murderer, Walter Turner, was a weaver from Back Lane, who had previously served nine months in gaol for attempting to cut his wife's throat. Turner was hung at Armley in August 1891; Barbara Waterhouse's funeral was attended by over a thousand people.

Lee Lane, c. 1910.

Cuckoo Steps, Newlay Road, c. 1960.

Construction of the railway bridge over the new Leeds Ring Road, 1930s.

Hall Lane during the 1880s.

Cookridge Beck (Fleggy Beck) in the 1930s. Dams were often constructed by local children in the summer months to create their own swimming pool.

Kerry Street, *c.* 1920.